Brian Webb & Peyton Skipwith

E McKnight Kauffer
DESIGN

Antique Collectors' Club

Design Series Format by Brian Webb
Design: E McKnight Kauffer © 2007 Brian Webb and Peyton Skipwith
Illustrations © Estate of Edward McKnight Kauffer 2007 Reproduced with kind permission
Foreword © 2007 David Gentleman

ISBN 978-1-85149-520-7

British Library cataloguing-in-Publication Data
A catalogue record for this book is available from the British Library

Antique Collectors' Club
www.antiquecollectorsclub.com

Sandy Lane, Old Martlesham,
Woodbridge, Suffolk IP12 4SD, UK
Tel: 01394 389950 Fax: 01394 389999
Email: info@antique-acc.com
or
Eastworks, 116 Pleasant Street - Suite 18
Easthampton, MA 01027, USA
Tel: (413) 529 0861 Fax: (413) 529 0862
Email: info@antiquecc.com

Acknowledgments
With thanks to Simon Rendall, Karen and Paul Rennie, Patrick Rylands, James L Gordon
Collinge & Clark, Robert Keenan and Bonhams 1793

Picture credits
© The American Museum in Britain, Bath, UK, pp. 38(top), 90, 92/93/94
London's Transport Museum © Transport for London, pp. 14, 36/37, 70(top)
© Onslows Auctions, pp. 71(top)
Shell Art Collection © Simon Rendall, pp. 23, 80/81

The cover and title page Communication illustration is reproduced from
McKnight Kauffer's Great James Street, London letterheading, 1931
The endpapers are reproduced from The Cornish Riviera, Great Western Railways

Published by Antique Collectors' Club, Woodbridge, England
Design by Webb & Webb Design Limited, London
Printed and bound in China

Foreword

Kauffer's images evoke for me my childhood, partly because so many of them are about the open-air, trees and hills and country landscapes of London's countryside, in which I lived, within cycling distance of such Kauffer poster subjects as Epping Forest and the Chilterns; partly because of their associations with Shell, where my father worked; but also because some of their motifs and techniques remind me of my father's own posters, some of them – as I now see – done under Kauffer's clear influence.

Kauffer was one of my father's few great graphic heroes (the other was Cassandre). He and my father were about the same age, and immigrants, Kauffer from Montana, my father from Glasgow, and they shared similarly humble roots; both had trained as painters but then learned how to design on the hoof, by getting on with it. They would have met frequently in the Shell-Mex design studio in the Strand, where my father was the senior artist, under the supremo Jack Beddington. Shell posters were then at their zenith and a steady stream of painters and writers like Nash, Piper, Sutherland, Freedman and Betjeman came in to talk about jobs. Beddington was brilliant but exacting: he made my father paint three painstaking versions of his Ayot St Lawrence poster, sitting in the churchyard painting with Bernard Shaw appearing now and then in the distance, before Beddington thought he'd got it right. When I was still a small boy, my father sometimes used to take me to the Shell studio for a treat. The studio was high up in Shell-Mex House, looking down on the Thames from somewhere near the clock. The big room was light and airy, with tall grey-painted wooden stools and the kind of easels that architects then worked at, and Shell posters on the walls. Later on, when I was nineteen and doing national service as an Education Corps sergeant (teaching trainee sergeants-to-be how to make their own simple posters), my father sent me rolls of old Shell posters – Sutherlands and Nashes and Kauffers – to hang up in my own highly un-military Cornish art room.

The Kauffer images I remember from those childhood and student years include the book cover and jacket for Herbert Read's Art Now; and later, the Shell

From a Woodcut   "Flight"   By E. McKnight Kauffer

Kauffer's Vorticist woodcut *Flight*, c.1916, was illustrated as a design for a poster in *Colour* magazine in January 1917 and in volume 1 number 1 of *The Apple* magazine in 1920. Kauffer was a member of the London Group allied to Wyndham Lewis, the founder of Vorticism, England's first revolutionary abstract art movement. The poster design was bought by Francis Meynell to launch the *Daily Herald* in 1919 with the copy line 'Soaring to Success! – the Early Bird!' The image which perfectly matched the aspirations of the new post-war Labour newspaper undoubtedly directed Kauffer's interest towards commercial design

★ ★ ★

posters including the splendid BP Ethyl controls horse-power, blue and white on a black background, using a photograph of sculpture. British posters before Kauffer had been dominated by draughtsmen: the Beggarstaffs, Brangwyn, Purvis, Hassall. Even Bawden's beautifully designed linocuts for his London Transport posters were equally splendidly drawn. But Kauffer was not primarily a draughtsman. He didn't observe things as much as create them. Even his strongest pictorial images, like the wonderful GWR poster of a white road crossing Devon moorland, seem not carefully observed but recreated, formalised, out of his head or from his memory, with all the unnecessary bits left out. That is why, whether one regards them as pictures or designs, they are so simple and unforgettable.

So was Kauffer an artist or a designer? Then the two activities were less rigidly polarised than they are now, and poster design, now virtually defunct, provided a half-way house between them. His work was stylish and formalised but not obscure - 'modern' but not unduly difficult to understand. Technically Kauffer was something of a chameleon: graphically resourceful, wide-ranging, skilled in various media, gouache, dry brush, stencil brushes and stencil-paper masks, and what in the innocently pre-digital '30s he called the 'scientific tools of T-squares and compasses' but generally avoiding the mechanical appeal of the airbrush. In graphic style his work ranged quite widely, from the only slightly formalised landscapes for London Transport and Shell to the more adventurously geometrical or vorticist typographic designs; from his simple silhouetted lay figure for Shell lubricants to his Flight poster for Meynell and the Daily Herald and his photomontages; from the book illustrations for The Anatomy of Melancholy and TS Eliot to the ballet designs for Checkmate. But his hand is unmistakably recognisable throughout - even his Provençal holiday landscapes in gouache look like Kauffer designs. Whether he is labelled a commercial artist, a designer, or just an artist matters less than the almost poetic imagination and sensibility he put into everything he did. He was lucky to have arrived in England when circumstances conspired to make such work possible. And he was miserably thwarted when he had to return to the more nakedly commercial climate of his native America where there was little need for what he did best.

David Gentleman, 2006

★★★

Announcement card for the 1918 exhibition of the London Group. The group replaced the New English Art Club as a focus for current painting and sculpture. Kauffer, who had acted as secretary to the group from 1917, designing posters and invitations, resigned in 1920 in opposition to their adherence to exhibiting only non-commissioned art.

Design
Edward McKnight Kauffer

McKnight Kauffer, Edward Kauffer, Ted Kauffer, was, simultaneously, a leader of genius and a follower; a brilliant innovator and an absorber of influences: but, in his chosen field, that of graphic design, he was as near the top of the tree as any man, or woman, can be. With some people it is possible to point to an inherited gene, but with others their creativity seems to have developed on virgin soil, often in the most unpropitious circumstances. Kauffer was one of the latter.

Born simply Edward Kauffer – the McKnight was added later – in Great Falls, Cascade County, Montana, USA, on 14 December 1890, he was the only child of first- and second-generation immigrants. His father, John, of Hanseatic German descent, was a violinist and tap-drummer, whilst his mother, Anna, was the daughter of Swedish émigrés. He grew up in Evansville, Indiana, on the Ohio River, where his paternal grandparents had settled, but family life was not easy as his father was frequently away on tour for long periods with various itinerant and showboat bands. These long absences culminated in a divorce when Ted was just three years old. With his mother now having to work to earn a living, he was put into an orphanage for two years: an experience which marked him for life and set him aside as essentially solitary and introspective, characteristics masked by a genial and gregarious exterior. His boyhood was like that of many other poor children in the small-town America of Twain and Faulkner, as it was, indeed, in Dickensian England: fending for himself and earning a crust as errand boy, grocer's clerk, factory hand, or whatever offered. He was later to recall his early life as 'lonely, nostalgic and uninspiring.'[1] The one relief he found from his surroundings and the depression of everyday life was in drawing, a solitary activity that attracted him from a very early age, and enabled

★★★

him to escape into a private world of his own. He liked copying reproductions of Frederic Remington's bravura paintings of cowboys and Indians, a vital and still living legend that would not be transferred to the silver screen for another twenty years. Perhaps it was the intensity of these juvenile transcriptions of galloping horses, rendered so graphically, that enabled him years later to encapsulate the sense of movement, which epitomised so many of his great posters.

Kauffer's mother remarried when Ted was eight years old, and his stepfather, John Rees, encouraged him to pursue his evident artistic bent. After leaving school, though barely in his teens, he found employment painting the scenery at the Grand Opera House in Evansville, and later, like his father, going on tour with a travelling repertory theatre company, in the combined rôles of scene painter, barker and general dogsbody. It was whilst on tour that he met Frank Bacon, an actor with a fruit ranch in California, who persuaded him to come and work part-time, thus enabling him to have the freedom to paint. In 1910 Bacon moved East but, prior to leaving, found Ted a position with a San Francisco publisher, bookseller and art dealer, Paul Elder, who promised to employ him provided that within a month he learnt the English language 'sufficiently to approach customers without his slangy stage jargon'[2]. Thus, as his biographer says, he 'acquired not only a speaking voice of marked attractiveness and distinction but also a lifelong passion for books.'[3] Whilst working for Elder he continued his art studies in a disciplined way, attending evening classes at the Mark Hopkins Institute, an institution that played an important rôle in furthering the development of what came to be known as the 'California School' of painters and muralists.

It was at this time that the young Kauffer met the man who was to give him his first big break in life, as well as his distinctive middle name and, more importantly, those initials 'EMcKK' that were to become such a feature of English hoardings, dust-

★ ★ ★

Woodcut   E. McKnight Kauffer

Woodcut c.1917 printed in black on green paper as an insert in *Art and Letters*, January 1918. In 1917 Roger Fry introduced an exhibition, with comparisons to Cubism, of Kauffer's paintings and supported his work by offering drawings for sale at the Omega Workshops.

" Housetops "
From a Woodcut   By E. McKnight Kauffer

Housetops c.1916, illustrated in *The Apple* Volume 1
number 1, 1920. Kauffer moved comfortably between
the relatively loose post war associations of artists
including the London Group, Group X, Omega and the
Cumberland Market Group which included Paul Nash,
who, like Kauffer, worked as an artist designer.

★★★

jackets and rugs in the following decades. Joseph E McKnight, a Christian Scientist, was Professor of Elementary Education at the University of Utah, and a client of Elder's bookshop. In a rare, long, and ecstatic letter to his mother, written on 1 August 1912, Kauffer described Professor and Mrs McKnight and their daughter and told her how their friendship had developed. He recounted how the Professor had taken a benevolent interest in his progress, and went on to say that McKnight was now proposing to lend him sufficient money to finish his studies in Paris; a loan, he said, which he would repay 'when I am successful'. McKnight viewed the money as a rolling fund that could be used again to help another promising student.

With the prospect of Paris in mind, Kauffer resigned his position with Elder, who generously gave him an exhibition to help raise funds. Excited as he was, he was clearly in no great hurry to leave for Europe, spending six months in Chicago, en route, where he enrolled in the 'antique' programme at the Art Institute, in order to study painting, anatomy and the history of art. He also exhibited with the Art Students' League. The timing of his sojourn in Chicago, however, was propitious, as, in March 1913 the Armory Show came to the Art Institute: taking its name from the Armory of the 69th Cavalry Regiment, its original New York venue, it was the seminal international exhibition of modern European and American art of the early decades of the twentieth century. It consisted of several hundred paintings and sculptures ranging from Delacroix to Duchamp, and included many works destined for American museums, which are now enshrined among the icons of twentieth-century western art. Few, if any, exhibitions have ever created such a furore. Its impact on the twenty-two-year-old Kauffer was immediate and lasting; at one fell swoop he had before him the whole history of modern European art from Classicism and Romanticism to Fauvism, Cubism, Expressionism and Abstraction.

★★★

Haunting the show, it was the paintings of Van Gogh and
Cézanne which immediately impressed him and influenced
his own painting style, but even at this early date he may
intuitively have seen the potential of Cubism and Futurism as a
vehicle for graphic art. He may also, in his heart, have felt that
he would never be able to compete on equal terms with such
giants as Picasso, Braque, Kandinsky and Brancusi, but inspired
by their example would undoubtedly be able to make his
own distinctive contribution to the art of the century. He was
ambitious and would never have been content to be anywhere
other than in the premier league.

He eventually sailed from Baltimore, reaching Venice in June
1913, from whence he proceeded to Munich, where he dawdled
for a further couple of months. Here he came, as if by fate, on
another of those influences that were to affect the course of his
life: the posters of Ludwig Hohlwein. Poster design had been
revolutionised at the end of the nineteenth century by Toulouse
Lautrec, Chéret and Alphonse Mucha on the one hand and the
Beggarstaff Brothers – William Nicholson and James Pryde
– and George Walton on the other. Walton's 'Kodak Girl' had
been a ubiquitous and influential image throughout Europe. By
the time Kauffer came to Munich Hohlwein's posters were all
the rage, and made a great impact on the still impressionable
young artist from Montana. The impact was probably all the
greater as Kauffer would have contrasted the effect of these
elegant posters, seen in an urban context, with the impression
he had received a few months previously viewing the great
works of Lautrec on the walls of the Art Institute of Chicago.
Art, he realised, need not necessarily be viewed only within
the hallowed precincts of galleries; it could be seen out on
the streets, a truth succinctly enunciated by Frank Pick in the
following decade when he wrote: 'A poster is to be seen twice.
Across a road or railway station it must have meaning and form
sufficient to excite a wish to see it closer. When seen closer it
must have further meaning and subtler form to awake interest,

★★★

Panela (unrefined sugarcane), 1918, cotton bale label from
a series commissioned for the South American market. The
labels, each measuring between 6in (150mm) and 6¼in
(160mm) in height resemble miniature posters, strongly
influenced by the 'Munich realist school' designer Ludwig
Hohlwein (1874-1949).

Oxhey Woods, 1915, one of Kauffer's earliest Underground posters commissioned by Frank Pick, illustrates the influences absorbed *en route* from Chicago; (the Armory Show: Cézanne, Gauguin, van Gogh and the Fauves) via Munich (exhibitions of Expressionism and Italian Futurism) to Paris where he was interested in 'everything', before leaving, as war broke out, for London.

so that seeing it closer appears to have been worthwhile.'[4]

He arrived in Paris during the autumn of 1913 and threw himself wholeheartedly into absorbing everything the city had to offer, working in museums and small ateliers as well as at the Académie Moderne; he was even inspired to begin a translation of Vollard's biography of his hero, Cézanne. It was the climax towards which he had been striving – Chicago and Munich were merely stimulating preliminaries. Although his appetite for work was prodigious, he still found time, though somewhat randomly, to attend concerts and mix with the cosmopolitan group of students attracted by the reputation and glamour of Paris. On 17 July 1914 he married a compatriot, Grace Ehrlich, a pianist who was studying at the Conservatoire. Their time in what was then the cultural capital of Europe was cut short by the imminence of war so that, after little more than ten months, his studies were curtailed, and the couple moved to England to stay with a Paris friend of Grace's, Maria Zimmern Petrie, who was living in Durham. She later recalled how Kauffer 'tried hard to find a market for his beautiful textile designs or posters, tramping the streets of Newcastle'[5], but lack of success made a move to London inevitable. Here, once again, he made a fruitless round of the advertising agencies before having the good fortune to meet John Hassall, 'a successful commercial designer famous for his simple, robust humour [and] his cheerful disreputable faces.'[6]. His work had helped popularise well-known brands of cocoa, condensed milk, furniture polish and Irish whiskey, and his iconic poster, *Skegness is so Bracing*, had achieved such fame that its central motif was incorporated into the civic crest of this east-coast British seaside resort. It was Hassall who suggested that Kauffer should go and see Frank Pick, the Publicity Manager of the London Underground Electric Railways and, as Christian Barman says, 'it did not take Pick long to make up his mind about Kauffer's stature as an artist.'[7]

★★★

15

Barman, who had been on the staff of the *Architectural Review*, before becoming Pick's assistant, commented on the ubiquitous recruiting posters by Brangwyn, Spenser-Pryse and Ernest Jackson, which were such a feature of the hoardings, before describing the impact of Kauffer's arrival on the London scene: 'In the middle of the war another very different designer made his appearance on the Underground stations. If the constant variety of subject and presentation had accustomed the public to expect surprising things in Underground advertising they were nevertheless somewhat startled by the forcefulness of a set of landscapes boldly modelled in clean, flat colours, the natural forms smoothed and simplified into a record of broad and arresting legibility. The artist was a tall young American, "a slim russet eagle" Sir Colin Anderson once called him, with a great shock of auburn hair, twenty-five years of age [...] In the previous year, 1914, he had been on his way back to the United States after spending a couple of years on the Continent. He had broken his journey in London, and presently he found that England did something for him that neither Munich nor Paris had succeeded in doing.'[8]

It is unclear at precisely what stage Kauffer had decided that his future would be as a graphic designer rather than as a painter of 'fine art', but, if Maria Petrie's memory was correct, it would appear that he had already made the decision, at least as far as earning his living was concerned, prior to his arrival in England. It also seems likely that the samples he initially showed Pick consisted of design work rather than pictorial imagery, because Thomas Griffits, the lithographic craftsman, recalled Kauffer's description of their first meeting and Pick's comment that it was a pity 'he couldn't do landscapes'. Kauffer assured him he could and produced examples to prove it, with the result that Pick commissioned *In Watford* and *Oxhey Woods*, these were soon followed by further commissions for *Godstone; Route 160: Reigate; The Heaths, No 178, Surrey* and *The North Downs*. E McKnight Kauffer had arrived and a new revolution in English poster design began.

★ ★ ★

Surrey, 1916, for the Underground Electric Railways Company,
forerunner of London Underground, illustrated in the December 1923
Commercial Art magazine which devoted the issue to Kauffer's work.
An appreciation of his work describes the 'essence of Kauffer's style
to be contained in the one word, Simplification. In this respect his
work may be said to have Continental leanings but there is so much
individuality in it, that any foreign influence has been obliterated by
his personal style'.

Despite this, he continued to paint, holding one-man exhibitions in London and Birmingham, as well as exhibiting with the London Group, for whom he designed posters, and with Wyndham Lewis and Frederick Etchells in the 'Group X' exhibition at the Mansard Gallery. The photographer Alvin Langdon Coburn wrote the catalogue introduction for his 1916 exhibition at Hampshire House, Hammersmith, whilst Roger Fry contributed that for his show at the Birmingham Repertory Theatre the following year. Fry noted Kauffer's struggle to achieve a 'just balance between his acute and delicate sensibility, and his desire for logical precision and completeness of statement.' It was probably the desire for 'logical precision' that finally pushed him into virtually abandoning painting for graphic design, but not before he had had one further exhibition in October 1921, this time in New York, at the Arts and Decoration Gallery on West 47th Street.

In contrast to America, where he was little known at this period, his reputation in Britain had been growing steadily in the years immediately following the War. By the time he returned from New York he had already made more than a score of posters for the Underground, in addition to those he had done for Derry & Toms, the London Group, Eastman's – a firm of West London cleaners – and his successful design, *Flight*, which had originally appeared in the magazine *Colour*, before being bought by Francis Meynell to promote the fledgling Labour newspaper, the *Daily Herald*. GS Sandilands in an illuminating essay describes Kauffer's analytical approach to the concept of a poster as well as to its actual design. 'Always acutely interested in psychology, Kauffer studied the processes of human thought with regard to the appeal of the poster. And the hoardings taught him many things. For instance, he frequently found while looking at an expensive poster that something in its colour or line-movement led his attention right into a crowd of other posters. In a word, he saw that one man was sometimes paying for the advertisements of another. Quite often, too, he noticed posters

★★★

that seemed to have the right impulse; but somewhere or other the impulse flagged and petered out. Advertisers were not getting their money's worth. Posters were not doing their job.'[9] Taking this distraction of the eye and dissipation of attention seriously, Kauffer set about making a semi-scientific analysis of the way in which people viewed posters and what held their attention. He decided colour was important to the structure of the design, and the design itself could best be expressed through the use of the simplest geometric shapes either on their own or in interlaced combinations. 'We live in a scientific age, an age of T-squares and compasses' Sandilands quotes Kauffer as saying, and continues: 'the attention, therefore, is attracted by the geometric, held by the geometric and geometric design is retained longer in the memory than the purely pictorial. For this reason, if the advertiser insists upon a picture poster, the basis of the picture should be a geometric one.'[10]

This exploitation of geometry, if not apparent in those early landscape posters for the Underground, became a notable feature soon afterwards, not only with the famous images for the Winter Sales at Derry & Toms, but also in posters commissioned by Pick advertising various museums – the London Museum of Practical Geology, Victoria & Albert Museum, Imperial War Museum, Natural History Museum and others. Indeed, the geometric rendering of crystalline minerals – 'stibnites' – as the central motif in the poster for the former, became a bone of contention during a debate on 'The Present Day Poster' at the Art Workers Guild in 1923. A Colonel Fraser posed the question 'Should the poster be decorative, and pleasing to the eye, or should it be aggressive?', Kauffer's *Uxbridge by Tram* and *Stibnites* being cited as contrasting examples of these two approaches. Kauffer held firmly to the belief that the symbol, however expressed, was the essential element, and he divided the public into two sections – the fast-moving and the slow-moving. Echoing a critic of an earlier generation who had defined a poster as 'something that is read by someone who runs', Kauffer preferred to design for the fast-moving, whom he considered to be far the larger section of the discerning public.[11]

Kauffer's exploitation of geometry, Cubism, and Orphism – as propounded by Robert Delauney – were also evident in a number of the book-jackets he designed during the 1920s and '30s, as well as in his illustrations for such works as Burton's *The Anatomy of Melancholy*. The latter inspired Roger Fry to write an article for the *Burlington* praising Kauffer's 'Cubisto-Cabbalistic forms', and commenting on his quite distinctive use of Cubism. Fry found the hundred-and-fifty drawings not only 'entirely delightful for their decorative charm, but peculiarly adapted to their purpose in relation to the text.'[12] *The Anatomy of Melancholy* was published by Francis Meynell at his Nonesuch Press in 1925. Meynell, who had spotted the potential of *Flight* seven years previously, was to prove a good friend, not only commissioning work but also renting him a studio in Bloomsbury. In return, Kauffer parti-coloured Meynell's car, as well as batik-printing an evening dress for his wife. In 1924 the Nonesuch Press produced the *Weekend Book* for which Kauffer designed a splendid dust-jacket in black, mauve, scarlet and orange, exploiting complex geometric forms inspired by the smoke and steam of a railway train. *The Anatomy of Melancholy* was followed by two other classics, *Don Quixote* and Herman Melville's *Benito Cereno*. Meynell had these printed at Plaistow using the pochoir technique of hand-coloured stencilling for which the Curwen Press was renowned. The colouring was done by a team of highly-skilled girls and was usually in watercolour, but for two others of Kauffer's books – *Robinson Crusoe*, published by Etchells and Macdonald, and Arnold Bennett's *Elsie and the Child* for Cassell – they used gouache, giving the illustrations a unique richness and depth.

Harold Monro, whose poem *Weekend* was the inspiration for the jacket of the 1924 *Week-end Book*, commissioned a signboard for his Poetry Bookshop, as well as getting Kauffer to illustrate T S Eliot's *Doris's Dream Songs*. Although Kauffer and Eliot were

The train! The twelve o'clock for paradise. Jacket
for *The Weekend Book*, 1924, illustrating the first
line of Harold Monro's introductory poem, *Weekend*, published by Francis Meynell of Nonesuch
Press, Kauffer's neighbour and landlord in Great
James Street, Bloomsbury.

★ ★ ★

already acquainted, being fellow-members of the Council of the Arts League of Service, their friendship did not really develop until 1927, when Eliot, on behalf of Faber & Gwyer – later Faber & Faber – commissioned the cover design and an illustration for his own poem *The Journey of the Magi*, the first of the firm's series of 'Ariel Poems'. During the next few years Kauffer also illustrated *A Song for Simeon*, *Marina* and *Triumphal March*, but his suggestions for illustrating *The Waste Land* elicited no response. However, their friendship remained close and during the years following the Second World War, when Kauffer was living in America, he and Eliot would address each other in correspondence as 'Missouri' and 'Montana', in playful reference to the states in which each had been born.

Over the years Frank Pick, Francis Meynell and T S Eliot became loyal patrons and good friends, as did four other men: Jack Beddington of Shell, Colin Anderson of the Orient Line, Stephen Tallents of the Empire Marketing Board and Eric Craven Gregory – or Peter Gregory as he was known – one of the founders of the Institute of Contemporary Art. Each of these shared with Kauffer that special relationship born out of the unique combination of professional patronage and close friendship. Jack Beddington and Frank Pick were the two leading commissioners of posters during the inter-war years, and they were men of outstanding vision and ability. Beddington came from a large family which had been connected with the arts as patrons and collectors for several generations; his aunt, Ada Leverson, was Oscar Wilde's 'Sphinx'. He believed that Shell should be marketed as a brand and set about doing this with energy and wit, commissioning a wide range of artists from Rex Whistler to Paul Nash. *You Can Be Sure of Shell* was one of the themes, but Beddington also devised a campaign based on specific professions – *These Men Prefer Shell* – and Kauffer created arresting images wittily demonstrating that Actors, Explorers and Magicians, all Preferred Shell. In addition to commissioning such works in his professional

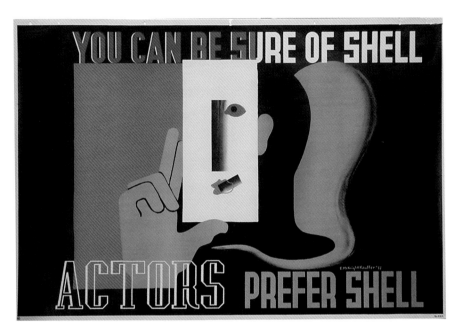

Actors Prefer Shell, 1935, lorry bill poster commissioned by Jack Beddington who was recruited as Shell's publicity manager in the late 1920s. Like Frank Pick, Beddington backed the courage of his convictions to commission work from the most *avant- garde*, and often untried artists of the period including Graham Sutherland, John Armstrong and Paul Nash.

★★★

capacity, Beddington bought paintings and rugs from Kauffer for his home, and the two men carried on a long and intimate correspondence, with Kauffer frequently seeking reassurance and moral support: 'I wish you were here…I need to talk to you.' 'You are always so sympathetic and good to me.'[13] are typical pleas from the 1930s, and later, when he left for America he wrote: 'I have tears in my eyes. I have a longing to be with you all, a longing that will never die… I miss not seeing you – but all our lives are now different so very different – England – beloved England – Devotedly, Ted.'[14]

With his wide-ranging brief at Shell, Beddington also saw the advertising possibilities for film, an interest he shared with Stephen Tallents of the Empire Marketing Board, which brought them both in touch with John Grierson, whose documentary, *Drifters*, was produced by the Board. The Board also, at Tallents's instigation, set up a Poster Sub-Committee under Frank Pick, and commissioned several posters from Kauffer in the early 1930s promoting such Empire products as bananas and cocoa pods. Kauffer shared their interest in film and helped found the Film Society in 1925; he also designed its logo. Apart from producing a design for Fritz Lang's *Metropolis*, his only actual practical involvement in film was his collaboration with Ivor Montagu on Alfred Hitchcock's *The Lodger*. He did have, however, some experience of the theatre, both with the Arts League of Service and in designing Ninette de Valois's and Arthur Bliss's 1937 production of *Checkmate*. Regrettably, the original costumes and curtains for this had to be abandoned in Holland during the War, but a revival was staged at Covent Garden in 1947. In the still intimate world of design and advertising, which centred around the Design and Industries Association in the 1930s, contacts were personal, and the key players tended to know each other, or even, in some cases, be related. Stephen Tallents's brother, Thomas, was a fellow-director of the Orient Line, with Colin Anderson, a serious collector of contemporary art, who was determined to bring the shipping industry into

★★★

the streamlined world of 'Modernism'. Traditionally the interiors of the big liners, which Anderson regarded merely as 'unusually large public vehicles', were fitted out by decorators, but Anderson was determined to have a sympathetic architect in overall charge of the interior design and fittings for the Line's new flagship, the Orion, and her sister-ship the Orcades. Many years later he recalled how he had considered several architects, including Edward Maufe, Oliver Hill, Chermayeff and Wells Coates, before selecting Brian O'Rorke, a young New Zealander, whom he thought would be more receptive to his own ideas. Kauffer produced posters, brochures, invitations, luggage labels and china for the two liners, whilst Marion Dorn designed all kinds of textiles; Lynton Lamb and Alastair Morton were also part of the team. For the Orion, in addition, Kauffer designed a large engraved mirror.[15]

Out of this group of intimate friends, the two closest were probably Beddington and Peter Gregory. In the early '30s Gregory lived at Swan Court in Chelsea, a newly built block that included a series of studio flats and penthouses on the eighth floor, which were much favoured by the design conscious; Kauffer and Marion Dorn were among the first tenants, as was another friend, the sculptor Antony Gibbons Grinling. Kauffer had met Dorn in Paris in 1923 and subsequently set up home with her, abandoning Grace and their daughter, Ann. Peter Gregory was a director of the Bradford printing firm of Percy Lund Humphries, and when the firm moved their London offices to Bedford Square, Kauffer designed a change of address card for him, using a technique based on Man Ray's 'Rayographs' – burnt-out whites and solid blacks. The Bedford Square building included a gallery where both Kauffer and Man Ray exhibited and, in 1935, the two men shared a dark-room which was specially set up in the basement for their use. Kauffer, ever conscious of his own early struggles, was generous to a fault in his encouragement of others, and gave Man Ray introductions to friends including Eliot, Virginia

Woolf and Aldous Huxley.

It is difficult to analyse Kauffer's character, but he clearly had certain chameleon-like qualities which enabled him to reinvent himself at intervals: the scene painter who had acquired a beautiful speaking voice, had transformed into the 'slim russet eagle' of Colin Anderson's phrase. A contributor to the magazine *Commercial Art*, Amos Stote – surely a pseudonym – wrote: 'McKnight Kauffer is a chemical composition. That is not especially significant. The same term applies to each of us. In the case of Kauffer the significance lies in the formula from which this particular composition was compounded. Even more significant is the fact that Kauffer has been able to change his own formula.'[16] In the same article Stote noted that 'Kauffer's ego forces him into eternal rebellion against the usual in art. His critical judgment sees to it that this polite rebellion is maintained. He lives his art. He studies whatever he does. His detached viewpoint regards his entrance into a room, watches over the pressure he gives to a handshake, concerns itself with the tone of his voice, prompts the words spoken, instructs his engaging smile when to make its appearance and do its work.'[17]. What Stote took for ego may have been little more than an aspect of the whimsical humour, which other friends recalled, or, more likely, a conscious front masking his innate diffidence.

If Kauffer's character is elusive, that was a matter of his own choice. It is, however, much easier, to appreciate his design philosophy, not only because the visual evidence remains as a testimony to his genius, but also because he did at times spell it out, as in the interview he gave to a 'Representative' of *The Studio* magazine in 1929. Although he was discussing the new rugs that he and Marion Dorn had designed for the Wilton Royal Carpet Factory, much of what he said could be applied equally to his approach to design generally. Context and containment within the allotted area were vital, as was his overriding belief in what he defined as concentric, as opposed to eccentric

Metropolis, c.1926 poster for Fritz Lang's 'futurist' film in which
humans are reduced to automata. The design, illustrated in
black and white in *Commercial Art* magazine, was described
'the most striking success in letterpress is of course the poster
for the Metropolis film. Here the overwhelming wheels and
giant piston-rods of the age of machinery together with the
Robot procession make a truly staggering advertisement.'

★★★

design. This theory dated back to his earlier study of the poster hoardings, and his awareness that some designs, instead of concentrating the viewers' minds on the all important message or image, positively led the eye away to other, extraneous, matter, thus losing the attention of the audience and doing a disservice to the advertiser.

With regard to the rugs, he related their design directly to contemporary architecture and the ground plan of the modern house, which, he felt, gave a 'structural sensation to the flat as well as the solid.' 'Take the new room as a whole,' he said, 'we demand nowadays that it shall be simple throughout. We require a plain treatment of the walls, and furniture that is treated simply in itself and is arranged in a formal manner [...] Now all these requirements of interior decoration have an effect on the floor covering. The eye turns with relief from plain walls to a pattern on the floor: which stabilises, so to speak, the whole appearance of the room.'[18] He then went on to comment on the fact that furniture was getting lower and that, although Gothic windows had been tall and narrow, and eighteenth-century ones square, modern windows were wide and horizontal, with the result that the modern rug should, equally, 'by its pattern, suggest the horizontal (which is also restful) characteristic of interior decoration.'[19]

Floors, walls, books and the stage were all grist to his mill as far as design was concerned. He was a modern man interested in new ideas and the possibilities of modern materials. The photo-mural technique invented by Eugène Mollo appealed greatly to him; he was a good photographer himself and had always been ready to use photographic imagery, when appropriate, in his design work. Mollo had perfected a method of projecting an image onto a wall and, through the application of photo-sensitive emulsion, fixing it there. The first public display of this revolutionary technique was in Wells Coates's Embassy Court flats in Brighton, where Kauffer's surrealistic design,

★★★

based on the sea-front and Royal Pavilion, was blown up and applied as a jolly decoration to greet the residents and their guests as they entered the hallway. He used the same method, but in a more overtly photographic manner, for an exhibition of Frank Pick's at Charing Cross Underground station advertising Joseph Emberton's new exhibition buildings at Earl's Court.[20]

During the 1930s both Kauffer and Marion Dorn enjoyed considerable success, but with the outbreak of war commissions dried up and, despite a dispiritingly undemanding job with the Ministry of Information, he found it difficult to get employment. The fact that he and Marion had retained American citizenship, and were thus classed as 'aliens', added to their difficulties, and Kauffer's Germanic name can not have helped, so, somewhat impulsively, they sailed for America on the SS *Washington* on 1 July 1940. Peter Gregory took over their flat in Swan Court and the painter, Hubert Wellington, took on the lease of the country retreat in Buckinghamshire, which they had taken in April 1938. New York highlighted the dichotomy of Kauffer's life; whilst in England, although perfectly 'at home' – and there was nowhere he loved better than the rolling Buckinghamshire countryside – he was conscious of being an outsider from the American midwest, but once back in the United States he knew that an important part of him had taken root in England. 'Some kind of buried masochism drove me insanely back' was how he described this migration to Beddington[21]. Hans Schleger was later to write that Kauffer had 'believed himself suddenly unwanted. The shock felled him.'[22] If this is not entirely accurate, there is more than a grain of truth in it and he suffered a serious breakdown the following year. The real tragedy was not that he had left England, but that he felt unable to return. His departure was followed by totally unwarranted feelings of guilt that he had abandoned his friends in their hour of need.

Although Kauffer's reputation was greater in England, his name was now not unknown in America, and had been

Strange Glory, the first American edition of L. H.
Myers' novel, 1936, published by Harcourt Brace
and Company. In a note on his working method
published in the catalogue of his 1937 exhibition at
the Museum of Modern Art, Kauffer describes using
'… toothbrushes, cheesecloth, wire netting etc. – in
fact anything that suggests interesting textures.'

★★★

considerably boosted by a retrospective exhibition of his
posters at the Museum of Modern Art in 1937. Work, however,
was in short supply, and what there was was more prestigious
than financially rewarding, and he was forced to rely to an
unsettling degree on Marion's earnings – they married in
New York in 1950 – as well as on a legacy she had received; a
situation to which he was unaccustomed. His exhibition, *Britain
at War*, was shown at the New York World's Fair in the autumn
of 1940, in addition to which he received commissions
from various publishers such as Alfred Knopf – an old
friend – Harcourt Brace and Random House, but for the time
being these were mainly dust-jackets rather than the more
prestigious poster designs. The desperation of his situation
resulted in large part from the fact that he and Marion had
abandoned virtually all their possessions when they left
England. 'I work every minute' he wrote to Anderson in
February 1941, 'I have none of my work here either originals
or reproductions – So I've had to make a portfolio of work. My
European reputation which preceded me by a few years has
definitely stamped me as English. This is not a criticism with
national inference – but a difference in the way of "advertising
thinking". The American advertiser respects the European
achievement but in no way will he admit it in American
practice – So I've got to wear that off! I've got to show them.
Shall I be able to do it? My American youth may now be useful
at last!'[23] Gradually things did begin to pick up and, thanks to
Bernard Waldman, the last in that line of distinguished 'agent-
friends', whose perspicacity brought his work to the attention
of an appreciative public, he received a generous commission
from American Airlines, for whom he produced more than
thirty posters between 1946 and 1953, depicting the allure
of destinations from Boston to California, from Mexico to
Scandinavia. His lifetime achievement was also recognised
in 1947 by the United Nations when he was appointed an
Honorary Adviser to the Department of Public Information.

★★★

He died in New York on 22 October 1954. Although the error
was not of Twainian proportions, *The Times* had reported his
'recent death' a few weeks earlier, publishing an obituary on
29 September, in which they said: 'He is to be counted *Primus
inter pares* of those artists who contributed to the renaissance
of British poster art after the 1914-18 War.' The identical
obituary was reprinted, without further explanation, on
25 October. Hans Schleger, an old colleague writing in the
Advertising Review, noted that Kauffer 'loved England but remained
American in fact and in feeling. As Laver said of Whistler "he
had something of the potted plant, transferred but never
transplanted."'[24] Like many another expatriate, his posthumous
reputation seems to have got stuck somewhere in mid-Atlantic,
and *The Times* obituarist's error typifies the confusion that has
beset it ever since. Percipiently, Kauffer had predicted this
thirteen years earlier in his letter to Colin Anderson when he
wrote: 'Perhaps it is an expatriate's (one who has withdrawn
from one's own country) fate to remain betwixt and between.
The mistake was in not being realistic earlier in one's life.'[25]
Although lauded as one of the supreme graphic artists of
the twentieth-century, both in Britain and America, he is
mentioned neither in the *Dictionary of National Biography* nor in its
American equivalent. Ironically though, Marion, who equally
retained American citizenship, and spent the last few years of
her life in Tangier, dying there in 1962, does merit an entry in
the British DNB. Such is fate!

Peyton Skipwith

★★★

1. Quoted Mark Haworth-Booth, *E McKnight Kauffer, a designer and his public* V&A Publications, 2005, p.9

2. 'Montana artist upsets another British tradition', by R Gram Swing, *Evening Post* (New York), 12 June 1926. Quoted Haworth-Booth, op. cit , p.10

3. Ibid.

4. *Commercial Art,* Vol II, No.10, April 1927

5. Quoted Haworth-Booth, op. cit. p.13

6. Christian Barman, *The Man Who Built London Transport,* David & Charles, 1979, p.26

7. Ibid, p.40

8. Ibid.

9. *Commercial Art,* Vol. 3, No.13, July 1927

10. Ibid.

11. See Adolphe Armand Braun, *Commercial Art,* Kauffer Issue, Vol II, No 14, December 1923

12. Roger Fry, 'The Author and the Artist', *Burlington,* July 1926, pp.9-12

13. Ruth Artmonsky, *Jack Beddington: The Footnote Man,* London 2006, pp.53-4

14. Quoted Haworth-Booth, op. cit. p. 97

15. See Colin Anderson, 'Ship Interiors: When the Breakthrough Came', *The Architectural Review,* 1967, pp.449-52

16. Amos Stote, *Commercial Art,* vol. X, No.58, 1931

17. Ibid.

18. 'New Rug Designs by E McKnight Kauffer and Marion V Dorn,' *The Studio,* 1929. Vol. 97, pp.37-8

19. Ibid.

20. See *The Architectural Review,* Decoration Supplement, February 1937

21. Letter to Jack Beddington, 31 October 1950 (photostat in the Kauffer Estate)

22. *Advertising Review,* Vol.1, No 3, Winter 1954-5, p.33

23. Letter to Sir Colin Anderson, 10 February, 1941 (photostat in the Kauffer Estate)

24. *Advertising Review,* Vol.1, op. cit.

25. Letter to Sir Colin Anderson, op. cit.

★★★

As with the *Flight* poster, *Colour* magazine offered Kauffer's designs, *above and opposite*, to prospective purchasers, commission free, in their 1917 issues. The magazine had previously illustrated Kauffer's paintings – a watercolour in 1915 and a still life in 1916 – and the Vorticist photographer Alvin Langdon Coburn reviewed Kauffer's 1916 Hampshire House Club exhibition saying, 'He is not afraid to use his paint just as it comes from the tube, which imparts to his canvases a joyous quality'.

★★★

Hatfield by Motor Bus Double Crown (30 x 20in, 76.2 x 50.8 cm) poster for London Underground, 1920. Kauffer's hand lettering is based on popular typefaces of the time.

Chingford by Motor Bus, Double Crown poster, 1920,
commissioned by Frank Pick who was also responsible for
advertising the Underground Railways Company's buses.

★ ★ ★

Poster design and miniature poster stamps for *Vigil The Pure Silk*, 1919. Kauffer's Vorticist influenced poster design incorporates the silk manufacturer's fabric patterns.

★★★

Winter Sales, 1922. The Underground's posters had the advantage
over other advertisers in having no competition on station hoardings.
And, by conveying an 'idea', the designer was not obliged to show
the 'product'. Kauffer's analysis of the poster hoardings led him to
believe that images with a central focus of attention would draw
the viewer into the design. In truth, like the Beggarstaff Brothers 25
years earlier, who wanted to 'frighten the carriage horses', Kauffer's
posters were noticeable by being startlingly different.

★★★

Eminent Victorians by Lytton Strachey, published by Chatto & Windus, 1921. Kauffer illustrates the subjects of Strachey's biographical essays with symbols relating to their lives: Florence Nightingale, lamp; General Gordon, sword; Dr Thomas Arnold, book; Cardinal Manning, rosary.

★★★

Original book jacket design, 1924. Pencil, opaque and transparent watercolours, for *Queen Victoria* by Lytton Strachey. The book was published by Chatto & Windus.

MURCIELAGO
NO   MTS   .   YDS

ARDILLA
NO   MTS   .   YDS

Las Palmas
NO   MTS   YDS

campo
alegre
no.   mts.   yds

dia de la
raza
no   mts   yds

bodas de
oro
no.   mts.   yds

LA FUENTE
NO   MTS   YDS

chorro de
oro.

EL LAGO
NO   MTS   YDS

★★★

Cotton bale labels designed over a twelve year period from 1916 for the Manchester textile company Steinthal & Company. The company exported bales of cotton piece goods to South America, Kauffer's vivid designs were more exciting than Steinthal's competitors' small black and white typographic labels.

Double column newspaper advertisements, 1923. Both Gerald Meynell, who hired Kauffer as Poster Director of the Westminster Press, and his cousin Francis Meynell, typographer at the Pelican Press (as well as Nonesuch Press and the *Daily Herald*), produced advertising for Shell–Mex. In the early 1920s Shell's advertising policy was one of constant change. Each 'season' (spring and autumn) the company commissioned new advertisements considering copy, name blocks and borders stale when a month old.

★★★

Cover design for the December 1923 issue of *Commercial Art*,
which reviewed Kauffer's work over the previous seven years.
The Eastman & Son *bookmark* was included as a loose insert.

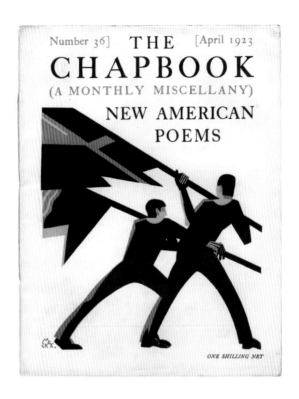

Front cover and back cover tailpiece illustrations for *The Chapbook*, April 1923. Harold Monro, the poet, publisher, editor of *The Chapbook* and owner of the Poetry Bookshop, commissioned Kauffer to provide drawings for his broadside rhyme sheets, illustrations for TS Eliot poems and a painted signboard for the Poetry Bookshop.

★★★

Eno's Fruit Salt magazine advertisement, 1924. The Eno's cockerel appeared in many different versions and sizes of poster including 16 sheet hoardings. In 1924 Kauffer 'arranged and edited' his book *The Art of the Poster,* published by Cecil Palmer, printed by the Westminster Press and its associate Sun Engraving Company. Although Kauffer's work at the time for Eno's and Eastman Cleaners was little different from current poster design, in *The Art of the Poster,* dedicated to Frank Pick, he took the opportunity to show his more modernist work for London Underground and the *Daily Herald.* His review of 100 years of poster design includes work by Toulouse Lautrec, the Beggarstaffs, Will Bradley, Hohlwein, Paul Nash and Picasso. He says: 'Contemporary poster design is fluctuating between a balance of inferiority and excellence just as it was in the eighteen- nineties. It is, in fact, at a similar turning point in its history.'

★★★

Calendar blotter, 1924. In 1925 Kauffer designed an office interior scheme for the advertising agent TB Lawrence whose company had bought the rights to *Flight* eight years earlier, before selling the design to Francis Meynell.

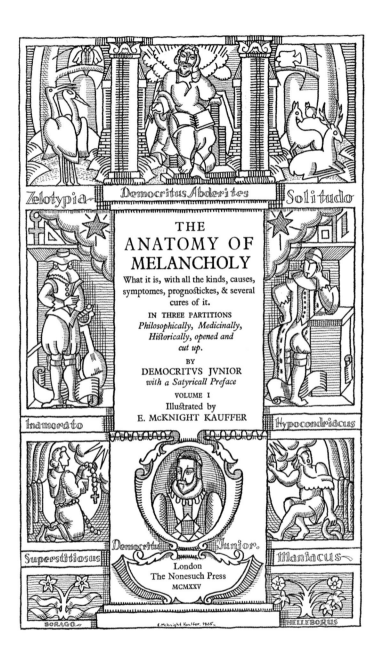

The Anatomy of Melancholy, 1925, Nonesuch Press. Kauffer's first illustrated book, the title page is an interpretation of Christof Le Blon's 1638 original. Commissioned by Francis Meynell the two large volumes of Robert Burton's text contain 150 line illustrations, combining wit and balance with Meynell's typography. Printed at the Westminster Press in an edition of 750 copies on Dutch paper and 40 copies with illustrations 'tinted in colour under the supervision of the artist' on Japon vellum.

★★★

Benito Cereno by Herman Melville, published by the Nonesuch Press, 1926. Unlike earlier 'private presses' Nonesuch was set up to make books with the ideals: 'significant of subject, beauty of format and moderation of price'. Still luxurious, rather than hand-set type printed on heavy hand made papers, its books were printed under Francis Meynell's direction by leading commercial printers including Curwen Press who printed 1650 copies with Kauffer's illustrations stencilled in watercolours, on specially watermarked grey laid Van Gelder paper.

★★★

The title page illustration to *Cornelian, A Fable* by Harold Acton, 1928
published by Chatto & Windus and printed at the Westminster Press.

Putnam 1925

Putnam 1925

Gollancz 1928

Gollancz 1928

Crime Club Inc. 1929

BBC 1929

Hogarth Press 1935

Hogarth Press 1939

The Arts League of Service was established in 1919 on the post First World War wave of optimism to harness 'energies set free after four years of destruction'. Wyndham Lewis lectured on painting, TS Eliot on poetry, and Margaret Morris, the League's *prime mover*, on dance.

★★★

POEM, "SISTER HELEN."
ARTS LEAGUE OF SERVICE, TRAVELLING THEATRE

The Arts League of Service Travelling Theatre, touring in a converted van was one of its best known activities. Kauffer's early experience of travelling theatre was put to use on set, costume and poster design, throughout the 1920s and '30s.

Elsie and the Child by Arnold Bennett, published by Cassell and Company, 1929 with 10 gouache illustrations printed and stencilled in an edition of 750 copies (100 specially bound and signed by author and artist) under the direction of Oliver Simon at Curwen Press.

The Studio, January 1929, introduced a new cover design by Kauffer which the magazine's editor explains: 'The Studio's adherence to permanent ideals of beauty founded on the classic tradition of the West is represented by a famous work of Greek sculpture, silhouetted against the symbol of the new age, the aeroplane, pointing upwards as if to soar to heights yet undreamed of'. To match the 'symbol of the new age' Eno's commissioned Kauffer to design an up-dated version of their cockerel – now a grape pecking black bird. In the same issue is an article illustrating new rug designs by Marion Dorn and Kauffer, made by the Wilton Royal Carpet Factory. Kauffer's designs *opposite* include a rug designed for their friend Madge Garland, the editor of *Vogue*.

★★★

★★★

Robinson Crusoe by Daniel Defoe by Etchells & Macdonald, The Haslewood Books, 1929, 535 copies printed by Robert MacLehose & Co at the Glasgow University Press with 7 full page gouache 'tipped in' stencilled illustrations.

Don Quixote by Miguel de Cervantes, published by the Nonesuch Press, 1930. 1475 copies in two volumes (575 copies for sale by Random House in the US), printed by Cambridge University Press with 21 full page 'tipped in' stencilled watercolour illustrations by Curwen.

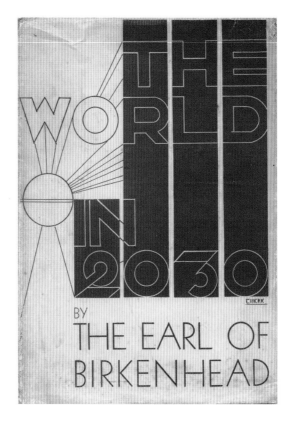

The World in 2030, published by Hodder and Stoughton, 1930.
The Earl of Birkenhead's collection of crystal gazings each
illustrated with an airbrush drawing, a technique that Kauffer
was not keen on, but thought appropriate for the subject.
Birkenhead (formerly FE Smith, Lloyd George's Lord Chancellor)
observed in his preface, looking back over the previous one
hundred years 'It may, for instance, be imagined that if the Duke
of Wellington had been informed that if within one hundred years
an American boy, flying alone, in a machine heavier than air
would cross the vast and stormy Atlantic on a non- stop flight. His
grace would have found it necessary to draw upon a deservedly
appraised resource in expletives.'

★★★

The world in 2030

War in 2030

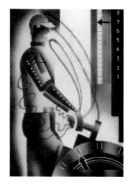

Industry in 2030

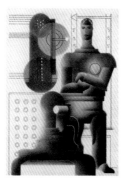

Everyday Life in 2030

The amenities of 2030

The air in 2030

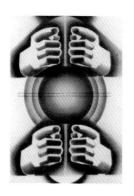

The world polity in 2030

Woman in 2030

The future in 2030

Faber & Gwyer (Faber & Faber) Ariel Poem booklets 1927-1931, illustrating TS Eliot's poems. *Journey of the Magi, A Song for Simeon, Marina* and *Triumphal March*. Eliot, a fellow American (they addressed each other as 'Montana' and 'Missouri' after their home states) and close friend of Kauffer, was a director of his publishers Faber & Gwyer (later Faber & Faber).

Personal Christmas cards, 1930s

★★★

One of a number of rejected original illustrations for *Venus Rising from the Sea*, litho printed key drawing with pencil and hand colouring. In a letter dated April 1931 to Desmond Flower at Cassells, Kauffer says, 'They are on the right lines but not quite right yet. They are nearer to what Arnold Bennett would like'.

★★★

Venus Rising from the Sea by Arnold Bennett, La Belle Sauvage
Editions, published by Cassell and Company, 1931, with 12
watercolour illustrations stencilled and printed in an edition of 350
signed copies under the direction of Oliver Simon at Curwen Press.

★ ★ ★

The Bright Hours and *The Quiet Hours*, 1931. Wyndham Lewis in his autobiography *Blasting and Bombardiering* commented that Kauffer 'disappeared as it were below ground, and the tunnels of the "Tube" became henceforth his subterranean picture galleries'

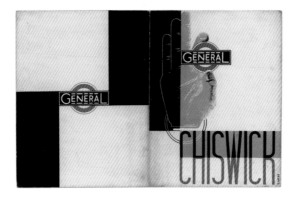

Chiswick, 1932, a booklet of photographs by Maurice Beck, printed at Curwen Press, with covers and layouts by Kauffer, describing the workings of the General Omnibus Chiswick Overhaul Works.

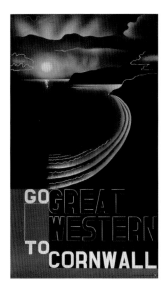

Posters for GWR (Great Western Railways) 1933 and the GPO (General Post Office) 1934, two of Kauffer's regular clients throughout the 1930s. *Go Great Western to Cornwall* is from a series of West Country posters. *Contact with the World* is also one of a series, designed to increase telephone usage.

The Cornish Riviera and *Glorious Devon* guide books, 1934, first published by GWR in 1928-29, with Kauffer designed covers and text by the well-known travel writer SPB Mais.

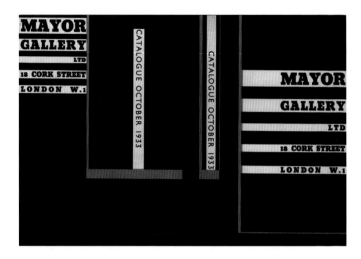

Mayor Gallery *Catalogue October 1933,* a survey of Contemporary
Art arranged by Herbert Read to coincide with the publication of *Art
Now.* Artists International sponsored *5 on Revolutionary Art,* published
by Wishart, 1935. The introduction to the book by Betty Rea ends, 'The
future of art hangs on the future of civilisation. It is time the artists began
to think what sort of future they want, and what they can do to get it,'

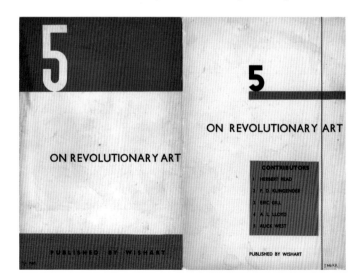

Regent Exhibition of 1934, organised by the Regent Advertising Club.
Catalogue for an exhibition of every aspect of advertising including
invited original work by 'famous people' including Kauffer, Tom
Purvis, Zero (Hans Schleger) and Eric Gill; the latest developments in
advertising including silk screen printing, portable talkie projectors
and three dimensional photography. Competitive sections included
campaigns, typography, photography and packaging.

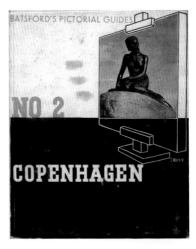

Photomontaged covers for Batsford, c.1934. Illustrated with black and white photographs by Geoffrey Gilbert. Kauffer used the easel drawing for his 1934 Christmas card, and again with his 'trademark' palette for a Shell, 1936, *Britain's Landmarks – Dinton Castle* lorry bill.

★★★

BBC, 1933.

Travelling Exhibition, 1934.

Union of Democratic Control, 1933.

Union of Democratic Control, 1935.

★★★

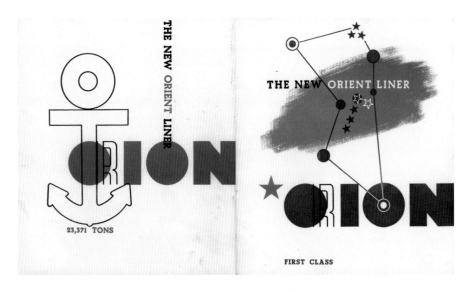

First and tourist class brochures for the Orient Line's *Orion*, launched in 1935. The photographic contents illustrate the ship's 'modernist' interiors by Brian O' Rorke and rugs by Marion Dorn.

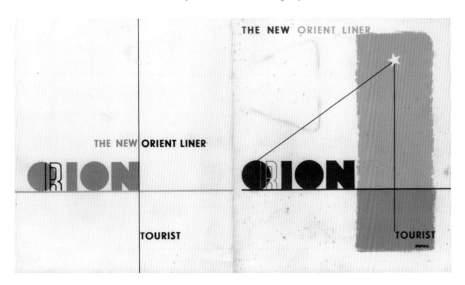

★ ★ ★

The *Orcades* was launched in 1937 and sank, torpedoed off
the Cape of Good Hope, in 1942. Kauffer's *Ships and Services*
brochure illustrates the Orient Line's Australian fleet

★★★

The Orient Line's symbol applied to a heavy-based vase, designed for use on board ship, made by Royal Doulton. *Opposite*, tie on hand luggage labels and circular stowed luggage label, lettered to indicate the hold in which it should be stored. Kauffer's and the Orient Line's other designers' work produced what was one of the most comprehensive corporate identities of the inter-war period.

★★★

ORIENT LINE

ENGLAND ★ AUSTRALIA

ORIENT LINE

ORIENT LINE

CABIN

Book through COOK'S 86. Oxford St London W

ORIENT LINE CRUISES

LTD.

ORIENT LINE CRUISES 1935

Printed in England

ORIENT LINE

The River Yeo and *Bodiam Castle*, lorry bill posters for Shell, 1932

Explorers and *Magicians Prefer Shell*, lorry bill posters, 1935

★★★

Exhibition catalogue, 1934, for Shell, one of Kauffer's early uses of photomontage, illustrating art and industry. The enamel *oil can* and *flag* badges incorporate Kauffer's 'oiling the joints' lay figure automaton which he had used in a prototype form in *The World in 2030*. The advertisement *opposite* was designed as a one-off insert in *Signature* magazine, number 5, March 1937, published and printed by the Curwen Press.

★★★

Programme covers, 1928–1929, 1937 commissioned by Peter Gregory, printed at Lund Humphries and an invitation to an exhibition of Lund Humphries' work at their Bedford Square offices, 1939.

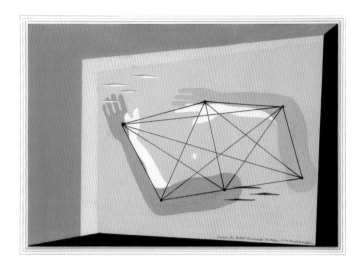

Kauffer's original sketch 'geometry of chess' design for *Checkmate*, 1937 for Ninette de Valois's Sadlers Wells Ballet and a design for a three-dimensional shop window display by Kauffer, 1931.

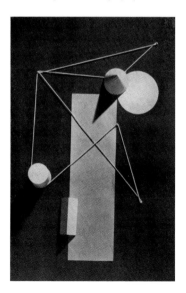

Liberty and Marianne printed cotton 'Friendship scarf', 1930s
produced in the US to celebrate 'America & France Forever'.

★★★

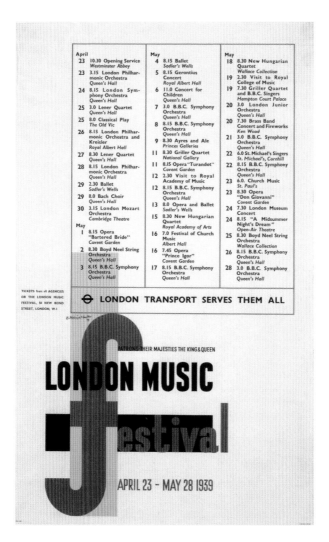

A Kauffer designed symbol, for the *London Music Festival*, his last poster for London Transport before leaving England for New York, 1939.

Kauffer's cover design for the London edition of *Harper's Bazaar*,
January 1940, incorporates a 'Lanvin black cloth dress with a white
sheepskin "button on front"', montaged into patriotically coloured
graphics. Although wartime conditions were beginning to hit hard
– visas, exit permits, luggage searches, reading matter confiscated,
delays – flying to Paris for the fashion shows, the magazine reviewed
Bacchanale, Salvador Dali's ballet with costumes by Chanel. Kauffer
adapted the cover design for his 1940 Christmas card. On 1 July
Kauffer and Marion Dorn sailed for New York on the SS *Washington*.

★★★

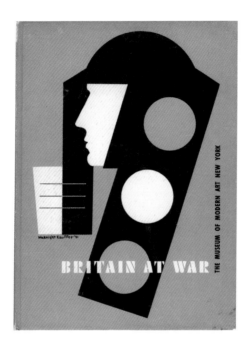

The *Posters by E. McKnight Kauffer* exhibition brought his work to
the Museum of Modern Art in 1937. *Britain at War* was added to
the British Pavilion of the New York World Fair in 1940, and in 1941
moved to MOMA. The catalogue, with Kauffer's cover, illustrates
the early stages of the war in photographs and paintings, posters
and cartoons. TS Eliot contributed his poem *Defense of the Islands*.

★★★

Posters for the Co-ordination of Inter-American Affairs,
Washington, 1942, and the Greek Office of Information, 1942.
As an American in England Kauffer was transplanted but not
rooted. The reverse seemed to him true on his return to New
York. War economies meant commercial work was in short
supply and commissions were largely for prestigious but not
well-paid jobs in aid of the war effort.

★★★

Green Mansions , WH Hudson's 1919, Random House novel,
reissued by the Illustrated Modern Library, New York with 9
full page lithographs and line drawing chapter openers, 1944.

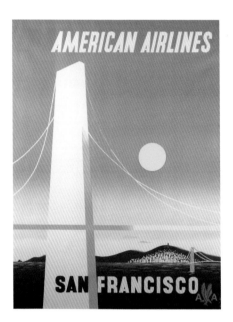

Kauffer and Marion Dorn arrived in New York without his portfolio
and with hardly any possessions. After designing wartime posters his
work for commercial clients increased and included an advertising
campaign illustrating every state in the Union for *Container Corporation*.

★★★

Between 1946 and 1953 Kauffer designed more than 30 posters for American Airlines. His work for the company took him across America and back to his roots. They re-established the romance of flight and helped re-invent America in peoples' minds after the Second World War.

★★★

Subway posters, 1947. After 25 years of designing posters for London Underground Kauffer had come full circle with his award winning 1947-48 poster campaign for the New York Subway Advertising Company.

★★★

Some reviews reprinted in the catalogue of Kauffer's
Lund Humphries exhibition, March – April, 1935.

'Looking around this collection one is struck by something basic and direct and
scientific in his work…The furious energy that runs through the whole show is
almost uncanny, If you could not see them you could almost hear them, and it is
one of the most interesting art exhibitions of the time.'
Manchester Guardian
'What apart from his ingenuity as a designer and his taste as a colourist,
distinguishes the work of Mr. Kauffer is the singleness with which he fulfils all
the requirements of the poster – arresting interest, meaning, carrying power,
formal unity, decorative appeal, and memorability – in the style of execution.
Those who have attempted proficiency in any art know that it is the crux of the
problem. It is easy enough to meet requirements separately, and then, so to speak,
to put them together; but to meet them all "in the act" means hard thinking
beforehand and then a complete forgetting, so that the technical act resembles the
discharge of a natural function. Mr. Kauffer's designs do not lie upon the paper,
they grow out of it, as if the subjects had been born there.'
The Times
'Mr. Kauffer dignifies all his work by his inventive design and his pure, bright
colour, and reveals a passionate honesty of purpose as well as a most uncommon
strength of drawing.'
The Sunday Times
'What is the reason for this success, and for the beneficent influence it has
undoubtedly had? It lies in the fact that Mr. Kauffer is the first modern artist
to recognise the artistic autonomy of the poster, and to avail himself of the
opportunities it presents; not, indeed, fitfully; not by way of relaxation or
experiments, but continuously, methodically, and quite exclusively.'
The Architect's Journal
'I have little doubt that E. McKnight Kauffer is profoundly tired of being pointed
out as a phenomenon. I am a little tired of it myself. But we must admit that
Kauffer is responsible, above anyone else, for the change in attitude towards
commercial art in this country; and it was the courage and aesthetic integrity
shown in his early battles with "the plain business man" that made it possible for
Kauffer to advance and eventually consolidate his position.'
Paul Nash, Signature, November 1935

EMcKK, Lund Humphries, 1935